Sleuth
ReadyGEN™

PEARSON

Glenview, Illinois
Boston, Massachusetts
Chandler, Arizona
Upper Saddle River, New Jersey

ISBN-13: 978-0-328-78990-0
ISBN-10:   0-328-78990-9
1 2 3 4 5 6 7 8 9 10 V003 17 16 15 14 13

Contents

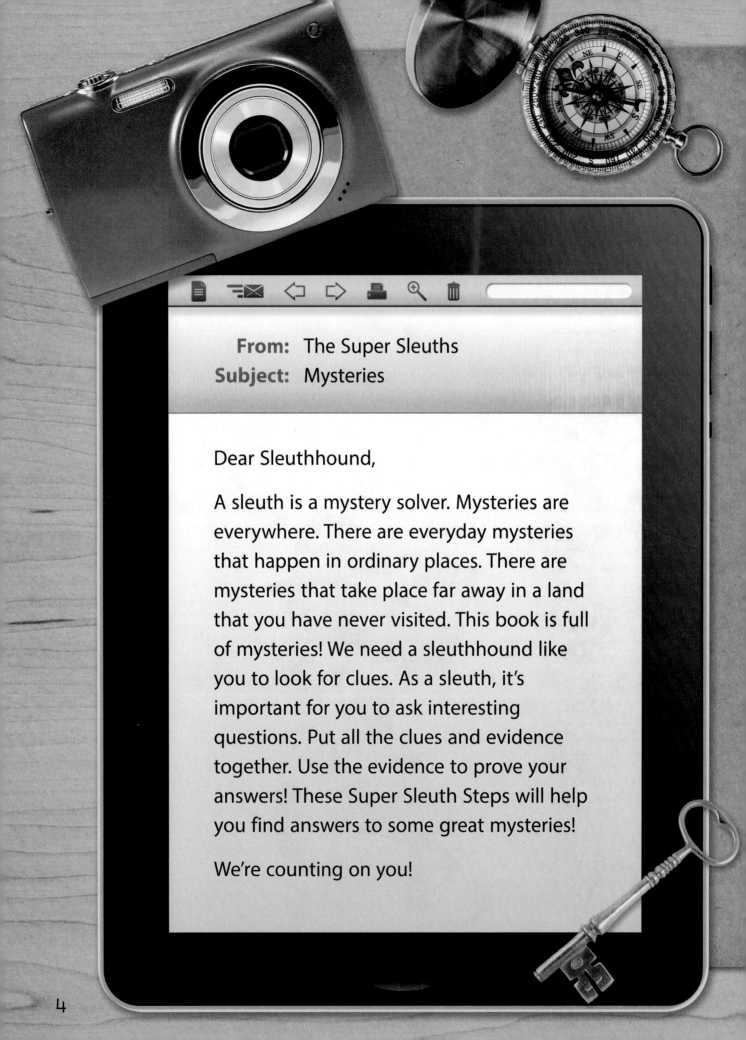

From: The Super Sleuths
Subject: Mysteries

Dear Sleuthhound,

A sleuth is a mystery solver. Mysteries are everywhere. There are everyday mysteries that happen in ordinary places. There are mysteries that take place far away in a land that you have never visited. This book is full of mysteries! We need a sleuthhound like you to look for clues. As a sleuth, it's important for you to ask interesting questions. Put all the clues and evidence together. Use the evidence to prove your answers! These Super Sleuth Steps will help you find answers to some great mysteries!

We're counting on you!

SUPER SLEUTH STEPS

Gather Evidence

- Look back at the pictures and reread the text. What do the clues tell you?
- Record the evidence. Write or draw what you find.
- Organize the important ideas. Try to put the clues together.

Ask Questions

- Great questions can be the key to solving a mystery.
- A sleuth is always curious.
- Keep asking questions. Questions can help you learn something amazing.

Make Your Case

- Look at all the clues. What conclusion can you make?
- State your position clearly. Be ready to convince others.
- Give good reasons to explain your thinking.

Prove It!

- Show what you have learned. This is your chance to shine!
- You may be working with others. Be certain that everyone has a chance to share the work and the fun!

Unit 1
Observing the World Around Us

Hi, Sleuthhounds! In this unit, you will be looking closely for clues. Here are some sleuth tips to help you. Have a great time!

Sleuth Tips

Gather Evidence

Where do sleuths find clues?

- Sleuths look for clues as they read. Sometimes clues are easy to find, but other times they are hidden.
- Sleuths look for clues in the pictures. Not all clues are written in the text.

Ask Questions

What kinds of questions do sleuths ask?

- Sleuths ask many interesting and important questions to find clues!
- Sleuths ask when, where, why, and how something happened.

Make Your Case

How do sleuths decide on an answer?

- Sleuths look back and reread. Then they think about what they already know.
- Sleuths put the clues together. Clues help them decide on the best answer.

Prove It!

What do sleuths do to prove what they know?

- Sleuths think about all they have learned and decide which clues are important to share with others.
- Sleuths plan what they will write, draw, or explain. Sleuths check their work to make sure it is clear.

Getting ORGANIZED

Mrs. Rodriguez asked her students to turn in their homework. Cora's stomach sank because she didn't have her homework. She remembered to do it, but she forgot to put it in her backpack. It was still sitting on the kitchen table.

"Cora," Mrs. Rodriguez said, "did you forget to do your homework again?"

"No," Cora looked down at her feet. "I did the homework, but I left it at home."

"I'm sorry to hear that, Cora," Mrs. Rodriguez said. "Bring it in tomorrow, but you will lose five points."

That night the phone rang. "Hello, Mrs. Rodriguez," Cora heard her mother answer. *This cannot be good,* Cora thought.

"Of course, I will talk to Cora."

"Cora," Mama said, "Mrs. Rodriguez says your missing and late assignments are going to affect your grade. That's a problem."

"I'm sorry," Cora said. "I'm always in such a rush in the morning. It's hard to remember everything."

"Cora, rather than being sorry," Mama said, "I want you to solve this problem. You're too smart to let a lack of organization get in the way of good grades."

"What can I do, Mama?" Cora asked.

"Let's think of some ways you can be more organized," Mama said.

Cora came up with three solutions to her problem:

1. Write down my assignments.
2. Get ready for school the night before.
3. Have Mama double-check my homework.

Three weeks later, Cora brought home her report card. Mama gave her a hug. Cora's solutions had worked!

Sleuth Work

Gather Evidence Cora has been disorganized for a while. Write two details from the story that let you know about this problem.

Ask Questions What questions might the teacher have asked Cora to help understand why Cora's homework wasn't turned in on time? Write two questions.

Make Your Case How do you think Cora's decision to change her habits changes what happens in the rest of story?

Lin's Lesson

"You know you're not supposed to bring food downstairs," Mom said to Lin. She was walking up the stairs from Lin's bedroom holding a plate of dried-up sandwich. "When you leave food out, bugs come, and I can't stand bugs. If you want a snack, eat it upstairs."

"Yes, Mom," Lin said, only half paying attention. He didn't see what the big deal was and why she was so worried about bugs. The few he'd seen in his room were harmless little ants. Sometimes when he was drawing, he got so preoccupied that he forgot about the snacks he had brought downstairs.

The next morning, Lin woke up to a strange sensation. He opened his eyes and saw ants crawling over his arm. Lin bolted out of bed. Ants were crawling on the floor and in and out of the pretzel bag that was open on his desk. Lin ran upstairs, where he found his mom drinking her morning cup of tea.

"Mom!" Lin howled. "There are ants all over my room, even in my bed! I never thought this would happen!"

"Oh, Lin," Mom replied, "that's why we have rules—to avoid just this kind of thing. I'll have to call the exterminator, and you'll have to save your allowance and pay me back. Got it?"

"Yes, Mom. I'm really sorry." Lin had learned his lesson the hard way! He would have to use his own money to pay to get the ants removed.

Sleuth Work

Gather Evidence Choose either Lin or his mother. What details does the writer include to show how the person felt?

Ask Questions Write three questions you think Lin and his mom would ask each other about this experience a week after it happened.

Make Your Case Do you think Lin learned a lesson? Write three details from the text that support your answer.

A Whale of a Rescue

Imagine walking along the beach and stopping now and then to pick up an interesting shell. You see something at the water's edge. You realize it's a whale—a whale stranded on the beach.

Some animals, such as seals, often come out of the water onto the shore. But for whales, dolphins, and porpoises, this behavior usually means that something is wrong. Sometimes the animal is sick, but sometimes it has just lost its way. Swimming in stormy seas can exhaust some animals. Their exhaustion will make them disoriented. Others get stuck in shallow waters when the tide is outgoing.

One time, in February 2011, not just one whale, but 82 were stranded! For reasons unknown, 82 pilot whales became stranded on a beach in New Zealand.

The Department of Conservation of New Zealand, along with over 100 volunteers, came to the rescue. They worked all weekend long to get the animals back into the water. All but 17 whales made it.

Then, just days later, 65 whales were stranded again! This time, the volunteers didn't try to move the whales back into the water. "New evidence suggests that moving stranded whales causes them a lot of stress and pain," Department of Conservation ranger Simon Walls told a local newspaper. Instead, the volunteers cared for the whales on shore while waiting for the high tides to return.

All 65 of the newly stranded whales were successfully returned to the water. The plan had worked!

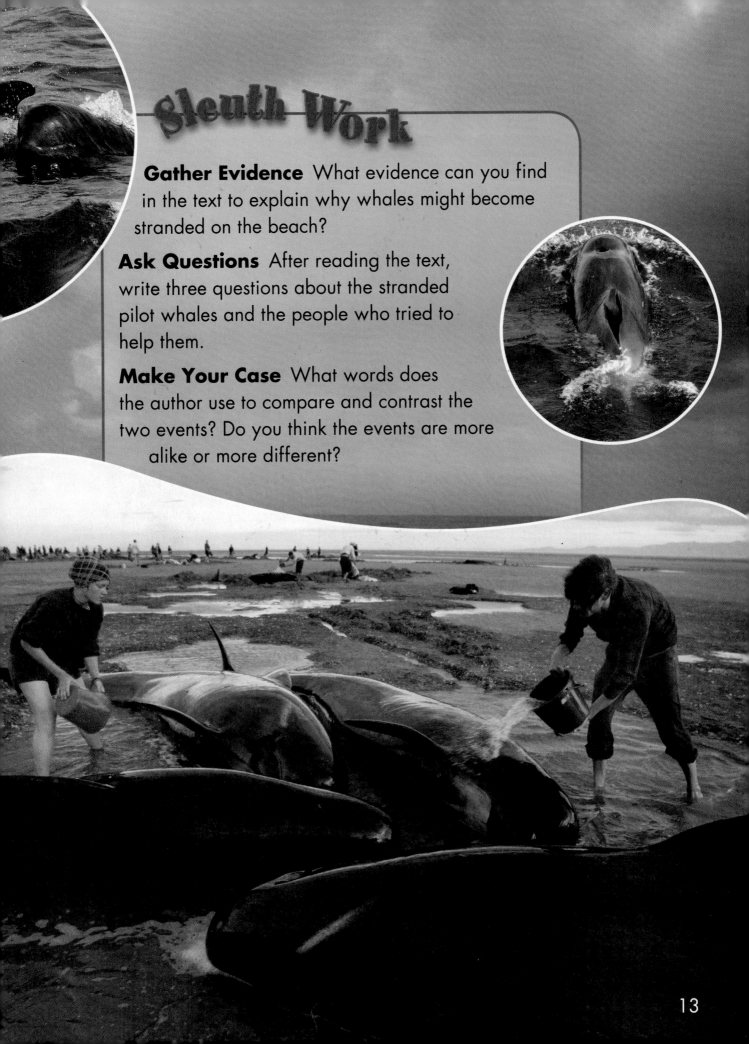

Sleuth Work

Gather Evidence What evidence can you find in the text to explain why whales might become stranded on the beach?

Ask Questions After reading the text, write three questions about the stranded pilot whales and the people who tried to help them.

Make Your Case What words does the author use to compare and contrast the two events? Do you think the events are more alike or more different?

BACKYARD SAFARI

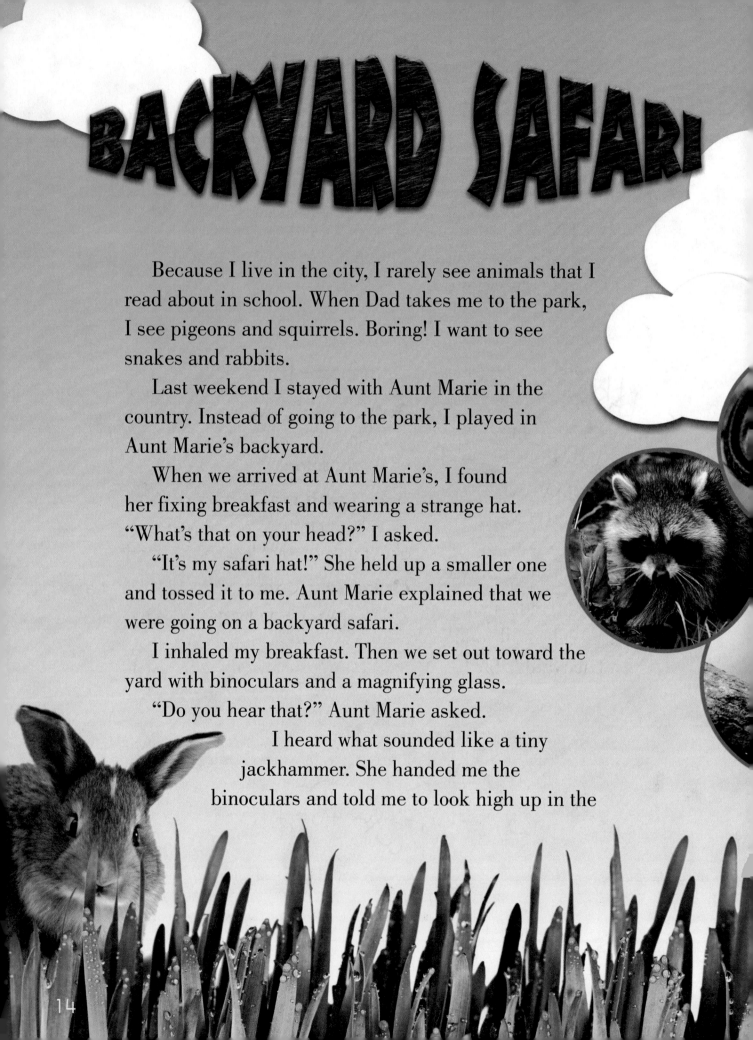

Because I live in the city, I rarely see animals that I read about in school. When Dad takes me to the park, I see pigeons and squirrels. Boring! I want to see snakes and rabbits.

Last weekend I stayed with Aunt Marie in the country. Instead of going to the park, I played in Aunt Marie's backyard.

When we arrived at Aunt Marie's, I found her fixing breakfast and wearing a strange hat. "What's that on your head?" I asked.

"It's my safari hat!" She held up a smaller one and tossed it to me. Aunt Marie explained that we were going on a backyard safari.

I inhaled my breakfast. Then we set out toward the yard with binoculars and a magnifying glass.

"Do you hear that?" Aunt Marie asked.

I heard what sounded like a tiny jackhammer. She handed me the binoculars and told me to look high up in the tree. I soon found the source of the noise. It was a woodpecker with a red head.

Aunt Marie said that rabbits love to rest under her rose bushes. We lay in the grass and waited. As we waited, she told me all about the critters that call her backyard home—opossum, raccoons, chipmunks, and snakes. Some like to come out early in the morning, others at night.

Then something caught my eye. It was a ball of fur with a nose that was wiggling. "A rabbit," I whispered, even though I wanted to yell. Who knew I could see so much wildlife on a backyard safari!

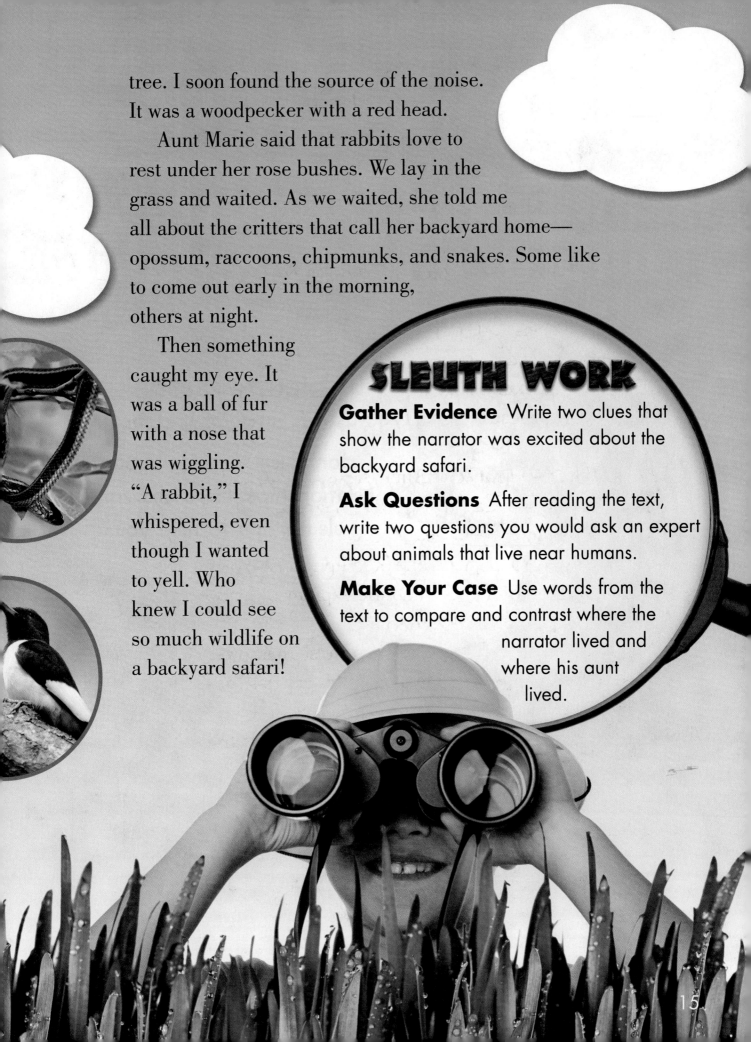

SLEUTH WORK

Gather Evidence Write two clues that show the narrator was excited about the backyard safari.

Ask Questions After reading the text, write two questions you would ask an expert about animals that live near humans.

Make Your Case Use words from the text to compare and contrast where the narrator lived and where his aunt lived.

Unit 2

Connecting Character, Culture, and Community

Hello, Sleuthhounds!

In this unit, you will be looking for clues to learn about relationships. Here are some sleuth tips to help you. Ready, set, go!

16

Sleuth Tips

Gather Evidence

Why do sleuths reread?
- Sleuths reread because they know that they may miss something the first time.
- Sleuths focus on finding clues when they reread.

Ask Questions

What makes a great question?
- Sleuths know that a great question should be focused on the topic.
- Sleuths choose their words carefully to make certain their questions are clear.

Make Your Case

How do sleuths make a clear case?
- Sleuths make a clear case by using the clues they found in the text.
- Sleuths clearly state what they believe is the answer at the beginning. They state it again at the end.

Prove It!

What do sleuths do when they work with other sleuths?
- Sleuths share their clues and ideas with other sleuths.
- Sleuths share the work so everyone has a job to do. Every sleuth is important!

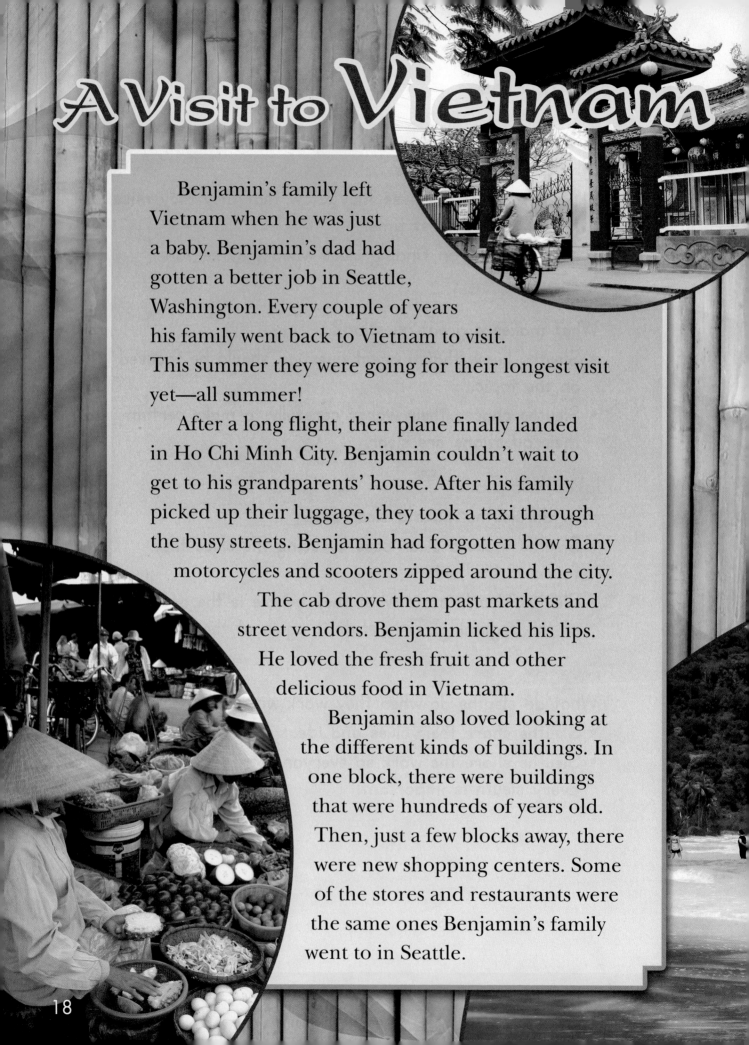

A Visit to Vietnam

Benjamin's family left Vietnam when he was just a baby. Benjamin's dad had gotten a better job in Seattle, Washington. Every couple of years his family went back to Vietnam to visit. This summer they were going for their longest visit yet—all summer!

After a long flight, their plane finally landed in Ho Chi Minh City. Benjamin couldn't wait to get to his grandparents' house. After his family picked up their luggage, they took a taxi through the busy streets. Benjamin had forgotten how many motorcycles and scooters zipped around the city. The cab drove them past markets and street vendors. Benjamin licked his lips. He loved the fresh fruit and other delicious food in Vietnam.

Benjamin also loved looking at the different kinds of buildings. In one block, there were buildings that were hundreds of years old. Then, just a few blocks away, there were new shopping centers. Some of the stores and restaurants were the same ones Benjamin's family went to in Seattle.

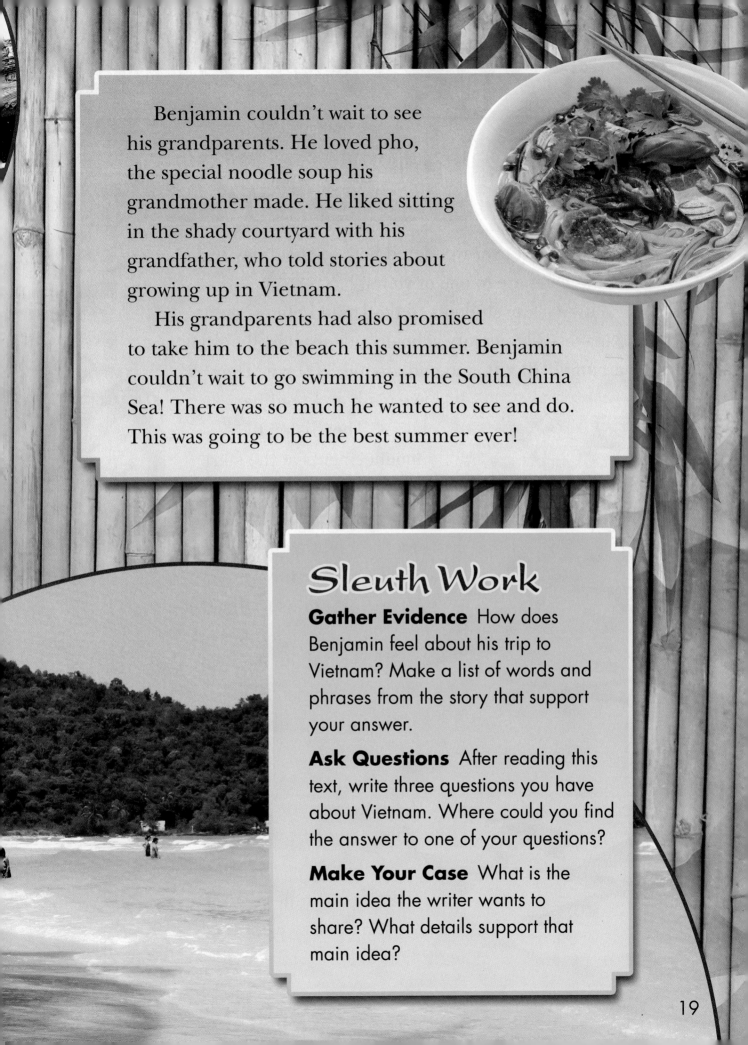

Benjamin couldn't wait to see his grandparents. He loved pho, the special noodle soup his grandmother made. He liked sitting in the shady courtyard with his grandfather, who told stories about growing up in Vietnam.

His grandparents had also promised to take him to the beach this summer. Benjamin couldn't wait to go swimming in the South China Sea! There was so much he wanted to see and do. This was going to be the best summer ever!

Sleuth Work

Gather Evidence How does Benjamin feel about his trip to Vietnam? Make a list of words and phrases from the story that support your answer.

Ask Questions After reading this text, write three questions you have about Vietnam. Where could you find the answer to one of your questions?

Make Your Case What is the main idea the writer wants to share? What details support that main idea?

A Day at School in Japan

Have you ever wondered how a school day in Japan might compare to one of yours?

Like many students in the United States, many Japanese elementary school students start their day around 8:30 A.M. and end around 3:00 P.M. They have math and reading classes. They listen to announcements at the start of the day. The teacher takes attendance. During the week, students might gather for an assembly where the principal or someone else talks to them.

There are a number of differences too. For example, in the United States, students learn handwriting. In Japan, students learn *shodo*, or calligraphy. This involves dipping a brush into ink and writing symbols. The symbols stand for words. Students in Japan also have a class where they learn how to cook and sew.

If you think school is hard in America, think about what students in Japan must do. They often have more homework than students in the United States do. They also spend at least six more weeks in school each year. Some schools also assign chores to students. Sweeping and cleaning the floor, wiping the board, and emptying the trash are some of these chores.

If you were an American student in a Japanese school, do you think it would be difficult to adjust to these differences? Remember, you would have to do everything in a completely different language too.

Sleuth Work

Gather Evidence How does a day at school in Japan compare to your school day in the United States? Write down evidence from the article to support this.

Ask Questions After reading the text, write three questions you would ask a student from Japan about his or her day at school.

Make Your Case What details can you learn from the images that support the idea that schools in Japan are different from schools here?

21

A VISIT TO CUBA

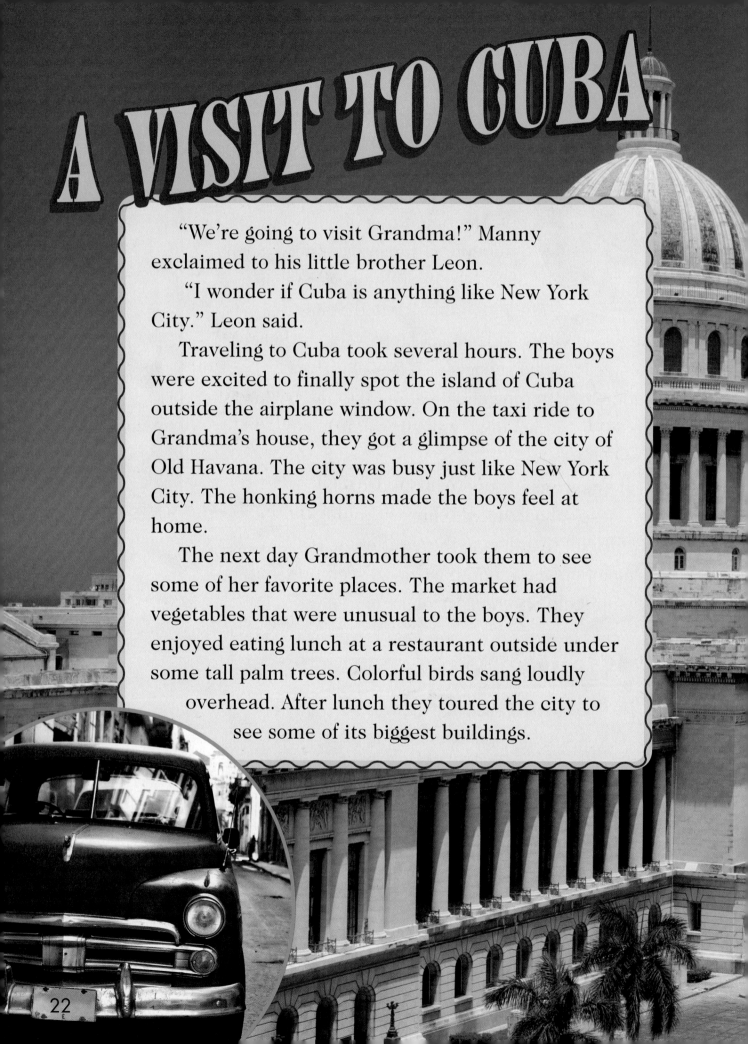

"We're going to visit Grandma!" Manny exclaimed to his little brother Leon.

"I wonder if Cuba is anything like New York City." Leon said.

Traveling to Cuba took several hours. The boys were excited to finally spot the island of Cuba outside the airplane window. On the taxi ride to Grandma's house, they got a glimpse of the city of Old Havana. The city was busy just like New York City. The honking horns made the boys feel at home.

The next day Grandmother took them to see some of her favorite places. The market had vegetables that were unusual to the boys. They enjoyed eating lunch at a restaurant outside under some tall palm trees. Colorful birds sang loudly overhead. After lunch they toured the city to see some of its biggest buildings.

"New York City has much taller buildings," thought Leon.

They stopped to listen to a band playing local instruments. Manny danced to the beat of the bongo drums.

After a week of fun, the visit had come to an end. The boys stood at the door to say goodbye. Grandmother said, "I have some gifts for you. They will help you remember your trip to Cuba." Leon unwrapped a special whistle that made sounds just like the songs the birds had sung at the restaurant. Manny opened a box with a set of bongo drums. "Now New York City can sound a little more like Cuba," laughed Grandmother.

SLEUTH WORK

Gather Evidence What details in the story help you to learn about life in Old Havana?

Ask Questions What questions would you ask the boys about the trip to Cuba that are not answered in the text?

Make Your Case Do you think Old Havana and New York City are more alike or more different? Use information from the story in your answer.

The World's Smallest Island Nation

What would it be like to live on an island in the Pacific Ocean that is only about 8 square miles? How is living on an island community different? How does it affect the culture? You might ask someone who lives on the Republic of Nauru (nah-OO-roo).

Nauru sits just south of the equator. Its closest neighbor is a whopping 200 miles away! About 3,000 years ago the first people migrated to the island from Micronesia and Polynesia. They lived in tribes or groups much like the Native Americans of North America did. Nauru had a unique culture and enjoyed peace for centuries.

In 1798, a British captain of a whaling ship saw Nauru on his way to China. Later, the first Europeans arrived. They brought new ideas, weapons, and war. From the 1800s to the mid-1900s, different European countries, Japan, and Australia took control of Nauru.

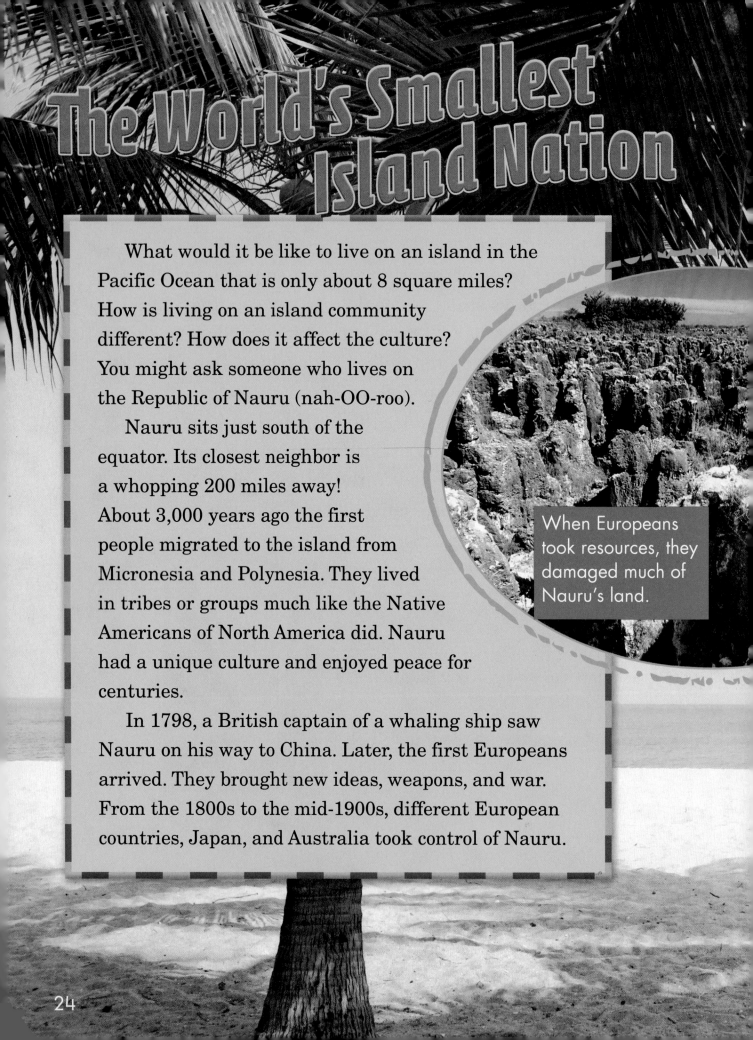

When Europeans took resources, they damaged much of Nauru's land.

They used its resources for trade and influenced Nauru's culture and community. Finally, Nauru gained its freedom in 1968.

Today, Nauru is home to many different cultures because of its history. More than half of the people speak the Nauruan language. English is also spoken, but less than 10 percent of the people are European. Other groups include Pacific Islanders and Chinese. As an independent nation, Nauru's culture is still unique. Its culture is traditional with a blend of other cultures from around the world.

NAURU

flag of Nauru

Sleuth Work

Gather Evidence What additional information can you learn from the pictures and labels?

Ask Questions After reading, what questions would you ask someone who had visited Nauru?

Make Your Case What are two interesting differences between Nauru and where you live? Why do you think those differences are interesting?

Unit 3
Seeking Explanations

Hello, Sleuthhounds!

In this unit, you will be looking for clues and finding some interesting explanations. Here are some sleuth tips to help you. Good luck!

Sleuth Tips

Gather Evidence

How do sleuths get clues from pictures?

- Sleuths use pictures to help them understand. Pictures can help explain harder words or ideas.
- Sleuths look at pictures to learn things that may not be included in the text.

Ask Questions

Why are sleuths so curious?

- Sleuths are always wondering. They try to find hidden clues by asking questions.
- Sleuths know that being curious and asking questions can lead to answers and adventures!

Make Your Case

Why don't all sleuths agree on the answers?

- Sleuths may find different clues, or they may put the same clues together in different ways.
- Sleuths know that everyone has different experiences. Our unique experiences cause each of us to think differently.

Prove It!

How can sleuths be creative when showing what they have learned?

- Sleuths are unique! They use new and different ways to show details clearly.
- Sleuths are creative! They think of different ways to share what they know.

We Need New Tornado Warnings!

Over 1,200 tornadoes touched down in the United States in 2010. Sirens are often used to alert people of the possibility of a tornado. I think tornado sirens are now obsolete. They should be replaced.

Obviously, it is important to warn people of danger. In the past, bells were hung high in towers to warn people. When communities began to use electricity in the 1930s, sirens replaced bells as the warning signal.

I grew up listening to the blares of tornado siren tests. They happened every Wednesday morning at 10:00. Clear, sunny days in the summer were suddenly interrupted with a deafening siren. I got used to ignoring them.

Also, tornado sirens can cause panic to people who aren't used to them. One time, a visitor heard the Wednesday morning siren test. She panicked. She ran inside for shelter.

There was not a rain cloud in sight. Such is the power of a tornado siren!

There are better ways to warn people about tornados. By the 1960s, radio and television were used as warning systems. With the Internet, cell phones, and smartphones, we now have a fast way of tracking a storm. This technology can even help you locate the nearest tornado shelter! With a siren, you have only a warning and not much else.

Finally, sirens can cost lots of money. Let's spend the money we save from not using sirens on sharing information. We can make certain that emergency weather information is communicated through the technology of today.

SLEUTH WORK

Gather Evidence What clues in the text tell you the writer is giving both facts and opinions?

Ask Questions What two questions would you ask a weather forecaster about tornados? What two questions would you ask someone who had survived a tornado?

Make Your Case Do you think the writer does a good job of stating an opinion and giving reasons to support it? Cite examples from the text to support your opinion about the writer's skills.

Taking Shelter

The first week of May in Tornado Alley was active that year. Nearly every day after school, Kristen heard the tornado siren from the nearby Oklahoma town. She rushed to her basement for shelter.

Kirsten's friend Julia had never spent tornado season in the area. She was staying with Kirsten because her parents were out of town. As the girls talked in the yard, the tornado siren wailed. Kirsten bolted toward her house. Julia asked Kirsten what she was doing. "Going to the basement!"

Julia stared at Kirsten as if she were crazy and foolish. She said that she and her parents never did anything when they heard a siren. Just then, Kirsten saw her mom frantically waving from the porch. "Come in, girls!"

In the basement, Kirsten told her mom what Julia had said. Kirsten's mom looked at Julia. "Let me tell you just how important tornado sirens are. This house is not the same one we bought. A tornado smashed the first one."

Julia's heart raced. Kirsten's mom explained, "That tornado had winds of up to 165 miles per hour. It was given an EF-3 rating on the Fujita (foo-JEE-ta) Scale. Do you know what the Fujita Scale is?" Julia nodded.

Kirsten's mom described the sound that the tornado made. "It was like a freight train speeding by," she said. Julia turned pale. She missed her parents and promised Kirsten's mom that she and her parents would take her advice. They would take shelter when the siren sounded.

Enhanced Fujita Scale		
Rating	Wind Speed	Damage
EF-0	65–85 mph	Minor
EF-1	86–110 mph	Moderate
EF-2	111–135 mph	Considerable
EF-3	136–165 mph	Severe
EF-4	166–200 mph	Extreme
EF-5	Over 200 mph	Catastrophic

Sleuth Work

Gather Evidence What traits would you use to describe each character in the story? Cite evidence from the text to support your choices.

Ask Questions What two questions would you ask a tornado expert? Where could you look to find answers to your questions?

Make Your Case What convincing information was shared with Kirsten to get her to promise to take cover next time?

Weather Work

Do you need a jacket today? Will you need an umbrella? Meteorologists help us answer those kinds of weather questions. Meteorologists are more than just the people on TV telling us what the weather is going to be like today. Meteorologists are scientists. They go to school to learn all about the weather and what creates it.

Predicting the weather is a big part of being a meteorologist. Today, meteorologists depend on technology and weather observers around the world to help them.

Weather observers are very important to meteorologists. These observers make measurements every day at nearly 10,000 different weather stations. Thousands of ships at sea record the weather also. More than 500 weather stations release weather balloons. The balloons collect weather data. All of this data is closely examined. Then the data is used to make weather predictions.

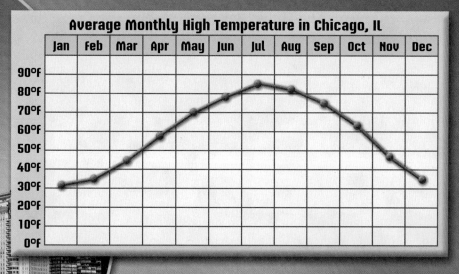

Average Monthly High Temperature in Chicago, IL

Being a meteorologist is an important job! Meteorologists help us stay safe during dangerous weather. They work with city managers to plan the number of snowplows needed during winter storms. They provide information to power companies. This helps the companies meet energy needs during hot or cold spells. They even help sporting event organizers predict whether a game can go on after a rain delay.

The next time you watch a meteorologist on TV, keep in mind that the two-minute weather forecast is based on hours of research. Three cheers for meteorologists!

Sleuth Work

Gather Evidence What clues can you find that tell you the writer's opinion about meteorologists? Make a list of these words.

Ask Questions Write three questions to ask someone in your class using the information on the graph.

Be Prepared!

Are you ready for an emergency? In school, you prepare with practice drills in case of a fire, tornado, or hurricane. Do you practice being ready for an emergency at home?

You need to put together an emergency kit! This kit should always be kept in a place at home that is easy to remember and find. If disaster hits, the emergency kit should supply you with everything you need. You should be prepared to be without electricity or water for a couple of days.

One of the most important supplies in an emergency kit is water. You'll need one gallon of water per person in your family for at least three days. You should also have three days' worth of food. Food needs to be nonperishable. That means food that cannot spoil. Foods like granola bars, canned tuna, dried fruits, and crackers are some examples.

A radio that can be powered by batteries is also important. You'll need to know what is happening. Be sure to have extra batteries in your emergency supply kit too. Flashlights, a whistle to signal for help, and a first-aid kit are also very important.

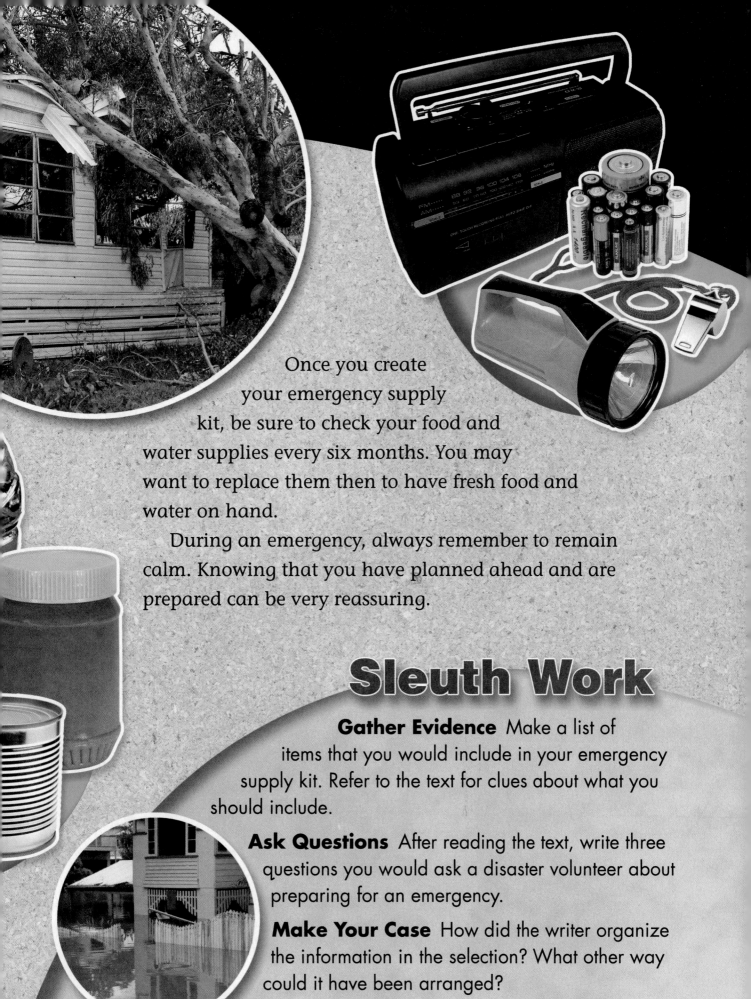

Once you create your emergency supply kit, be sure to check your food and water supplies every six months. You may want to replace them then to have fresh food and water on hand.

During an emergency, always remember to remain calm. Knowing that you have planned ahead and are prepared can be very reassuring.

Sleuth Work

Gather Evidence Make a list of items that you would include in your emergency supply kit. Refer to the text for clues about what you should include.

Ask Questions After reading the text, write three questions you would ask a disaster volunteer about preparing for an emergency.

Make Your Case How did the writer organize the information in the selection? What other way could it have been arranged?

Unit 4

Becoming an Active Citizen

Hi, Sleuthhounds!

In this unit, you will be looking for clues about some involved citizens. Here are some sleuth tips to help you. Be unique!

Sleuth Tips

Gather Evidence

How do sleuths remember clues?

- Sleuths don't expect to remember everything they read and see. They write down important details.
- Sleuths might write a list or draw a picture to help them remember clues.

Ask Questions

Why do sleuths ask questions?

- Sleuths ask questions to gather facts and details about a topic.
- Sleuths ask questions to make everyone think harder or differently.

Make Your Case

How do sleuths disagree with other sleuths?

- Sleuths know that everyone is unique and that not everyone will agree. They want to hear lots of ideas.
- Sleuths discuss clues with others to find areas of agreement.

Prove It!

What do sleuths think about before they share?

- Sleuths review what they have learned before they present it.
- Sleuths consider what is most important to include and what can be left out.

Don't Give Up!

What do Sonia Sotomayor, Walt Disney, Dr. Seuss, and Thomas Edison have in common? They have become famous, successful people—but they didn't start out that way!

Sonia Sotomayor has overcome many challenges. She grew up poor and lost her father when she was young. She spoke only Spanish as a child. However, she studied hard in school and became a lawyer. Today she serves on the United States Supreme Court. She is only the third woman to do so.

Sonia Sotomayor

Walt Disney was fired from his newspaper job and told he had a poor imagination. Today, Disney's ideas inspire theme parks and a movie company.

Theodor Geisel, also known as Dr. Seuss, wrote his first book called *And to Think That I Saw It on Mulberry Street*. After 27 different book companies turned it down, one company printed it. He went on to write over 40 children's books.

These people might have just given up, but they *didn't*. They kept trying and became successful.

Walt Disney

Thomas Edison didn't give up, either. He invented many things, including a long-lasting light bulb. It took him hundreds of tries before he found the materials that worked best for this invention. He never thought of himself as a failure. He said, "I have not failed. I've just found ten thousand ways that won't work."

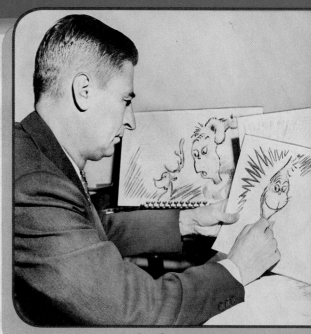
Dr. Seuss

Every time Edison tried something that didn't work, he got one step closer to finding a way that *would* work.

So the next time you're trying to learn something new or solve a problem, don't stop trying. You may be just one step away from success!

Thomas Edison

Sleuth Work

Gather Evidence How does the author feel about failure? Write sentences from the article that support your answer.

Ask Questions If you could talk to one of the famous people mentioned in this article, whom would you talk to and what would you ask? Make a list of the questions you would like to ask.

Make Your Case What reasons does the writer give to support the conclusion to this selection?

HONORING CODE TALKERS

On July 26, 2001, four Native Americans received the Congressional Gold Medal. It is the highest civilian award the U.S. Congress can give. These men were survivors of the Navajo Code Talkers. The Code Talkers used their native language to send secret messages during World War II. It took about 60 years for them to be recognized for their service.

Inside the Capitol in Washington, D.C., President George W. Bush addressed the audience. He said, "Today, America honors 21 Native Americans who, in a desperate hour, gave their country a service only they could give."

Bill Toledo was a Code Talker for three years. On the island of Guam, he barely missed being hit by sniper bullets. Thanks to his quick feet, he escaped unharmed. Later, while marching through the jungle, he was mistaken for a Japanese soldier. He was taken prisoner at gunpoint. The mistake was soon realized. He was given a bodyguard so it would not happen again. The Code Talkers were very important to the war effort.

Mr. Toledo said that it's important to share his experiences with younger generations. He wants them to understand that freedom comes at a cost. He wants them to appreciate the sacrifices that service people have made. It is these sacrifices that have helped Americans keep our freedom.

SLEUTH WORK

Gather Evidence How does the author feel about the Code Talkers? Write down evidence from the article to support your answer.

Ask Questions After reading the text, if you could talk to a Code Talker about his experiences, what would you ask him? Write two factual questions and two opinion questions that you would ask.

Make Your Case What does a reader need to know about World War II to better understand this selection? How does knowing about history help you to better understand selections such as this one?

VOTE

It was time for the school elections. Each class was supposed to vote on who would represent it in the school congress. A committee was formed of third, fourth, and fifth graders. Its job was to choose the best voting process. Everyone had ideas about how the voting should be done.

Anton, a fifth grader, thought everyone should fill out a ballot. The voting station would be in the school cafeteria. At lunch, each student would write a candidate's name on a piece of paper and put it into a box. Then the votes would be counted.

Nisha, a fourth grader, thought that each class should vote for a representative. Then each grade would vote for those winners to select a representative for each grade.

Scotty, a third grader, thought that each grade should have an assembly to choose its representative. Someone would call out a candidate's name.

Then students would raise their hands if they wanted that person to represent them. The person who got the most hands raised would be the winner.

The students went round and round about what they should do. Finally, they asked a teacher for her thoughts. "We're having a hard time agreeing on the voting process for the election," they said to the teacher.

"Why not vote on it?" asked Mrs. Hanson.

Vote for TIM

Sleuth Work

Gather Evidence The election committee had several ideas for the voting process. How were they all alike? Write details that support this.

Ask Questions When the committee asked the teacher for help, what questions might she have asked the committee to help it reach a decision? Write two of those questions.

Make Your Case Choose an opinion held by one of the students in the story. Restate the opinion and give a supporting reason to explain why that method of voting would work well.

America's National Bird

In 1782, the American bald eagle became the symbol of the United States. It was chosen because it's a majestic and strong bird. How did this bird get chosen?

After the Declaration of Independence was signed in 1776, a committee was asked to research a symbol for our new country. This committee included Thomas Jefferson, John Adams, and Benjamin Franklin. They presented an illustration of a woman called "Liberty" holding a shield.

Congress wasn't impressed. It turned to a Philadelphia artist. The artist's design included a golden eagle. This species wasn't unique to the United States. After some research, Congress chose the American bald eagle. Today, the eagle is pictured on our country's seal, money, and on many stamps.

Not everyone liked this symbol. Benjamin Franklin shared his displeasure in a letter to his daughter in 1784. He said, "For my own part I wish the Bald Eagle had not been chosen the Representative of our Country. He is a Bird of bad moral Character."

Franklin felt the American Bald Eagle stole food from other birds and was a coward.

However, Franklin was happy to see that the illustration of the eagle looked more like a turkey. He felt the turkey was a more appropriate symbol. Franklin believed the turkey was courageous in its own way.

Nevertheless, the American bald eagle still represents our country. President John F. Kennedy agreed with the Founding Fathers and once wrote, "The fierce beauty and proud independence of this great bird aptly symbolizes the strength and freedom of America."

Sleuth Work

Gather Evidence Write details that Benjamin Franklin used in his argument against the American bald eagle as our country's national symbol.

Ask Questions Now that you have read this text, if you were on a committee choose an animal as a symbol for your hometown, what questions would you research to inform your decision?"

Make Your Case What information can you learn that is only provided by the images and not in the text?

Acknowledgments

Photographs

Every effort has been made to secure permission and provide appropriate credit for photographic material.
The publisher deeply regrets any omission and pledges to correct errors called to its attention in subsequent editions.

Unless otherwise acknowledged, all photographs are the property of Pearson Education, Inc.

Photo locators denoted as follows: Top (T), Center (C), Bottom (B), Left (L), Right (R), Background (Bkgd)

Cover Chandler Digital Art

4 (Bkgd) Nightman1965/Fotolia, (TL) PaulPaladin/Fotolia, (TR) kontur-vid/Fotolia, (C) Kev Llewellyn/Shutterstock, (BR) Zedcor Wholly Owned/Thinkstock; **5** (CR) Warakorn/Fotolia, (TR) rrrob/Fotolia, (BR) Hemera Technologies/Thinkstock; **8** (B)Brad Pict/Fotolia,(T) Carlos Caetano/Shutterstock, (TR) Rob/Fotolia; **9** (B) Michael Flippo/Fotolia, (C) Stockbyte/Thinkstock, (R) rrrob/Fotolia; **10** (T) Judex/Fotolia, (TL) Hemera Technologies/Thinkstock, (L) Brand X Pictures/Thinkstock; **10** (Bkgd) tuja66/Fotolia, (R) Tupungato/Fotolia; **11** (CR) Photos/Thinkstock, (BR) Les Cunliffe/Fotolia, (B) Jim Barber/Fotolia; **12** (T) lunamarina/Fotolia, (BR) Skyline/Fotolia, (Bkgd) Tim Cuff/Alamy; **13** Tersina Shieh/Fotolia; **14** (BL) Vilmos Varga/Fotolia, (CR) Hemera Technologies/Thinkstock, (B) Nat Ulrich/Fotolia; **15** (TL) Alfrendo Nature/Thinkstock, (CL) Tony Campbell/Fotolia, (R) Nikolai Sorokin/Fotolia; **15** (B) Paul Hill/Fotolia; **18** (TR) Tinnakorn Nukul/Fotolia, (Bkgd) xiaoloangge/Fotolia, (BL) canakris/Fotolia; **19** (B) Jens Ottoson/Fotolia, (TR) uckyo/Fotolia; **20** (Bkgd) paylessimages/Fotolia, (BL) joanna wnuk/Fotolia, **20** (CL) paylessimages/Fotolia, **20** (T) Shutterstock; **21** (TR) Etien/Fotolia, (CR) japolia/Fotolia; **22** (BL) rgbspace/Fotolia, (Bkgd) kenzo/Fotolia; **23** (TR) Craig Jewell/Fotolia, (BR) dzain/Fotolia; **24** (Bkgd) Maria Skaldina/Fotolia, (C) Philip Game/Alamy; **28** (L) Frank Anusewicz/Shutterstock; (Bkgd) Rossler/Fotolia; **29** Dudarev Mikhail/Shutterstock; **30** Zastol'skiy Victor Leonidovich/Shutterstock; **31** Shutterstock; **32** (Bkgd) panthesja/Fotolia, (TL) Veniamin Kraskov/Fotolia, (CR) NASA; **33** (T) Henryk Sadura/Fotolia, (TR) flame&star/Fotolia, (BC) Ilene MacDonald/Alamy; **33** (BL) NASA; **34** (T) tm-photo/Fotolia, (Bkgd) clearviewstock/Fotolia, (C) Link Art/Fotolia, (TC) Anton Prado Photo/Fotolia; **34** (BC) MOKreations/Fotolia, (T) chas53/Fotolia, (C) Comstock/Thinkstock; **35** (TR) Nikolai Sorokin/Foto, (B) andesign101/Fotolia; **38** (BL) Everett Collection Inc/Alamy, (TR) Steve Petteway/Supreme Court of the United States; **39** (TR) Library of Congress, (BR) Library of Congress; **40** (Bkgd) Galyna Andrushko/Fotolia, (B) Douglas Graham/Newscom; **41** (TR) National Archives, (CR) Tech Sgt.Craig Clapper/United States Air Force.